Those Words I Felt That One Time

Dan Hart

BookLeaf Publishing

Presentation by *BookLeaf Publishing*

Web: www.bookleafpub.com

E-mail: info@bookleafpub.com

ISBN: 9789357214131

First edition 2023

This short volume is dedicated to the people I owe most for my love of writing.

My Nan, for sharing with me the joy of books from an early age. Without you, I would never have taken my first step along this path.

Russell, my primary school teacher through years 4 and 6. Without you, I would never have recognised the joy that can be found in writing, as well as reading.

Paul, my high school English and Media Studies teacher through years 9-13. Without you, I would never have been inspired to continue writing through my teens and into adulthood.

Rob, my best friend and Dungeon Master extraordinaire. Without you, I would never have learned to play Dungeons & Dragons, nor would I have fallen in love anew with the act of creating something personal.

ACKNOWLEDGEMENTS

My thanks to BookLeaf Publishing, not just for putting this book together, but for running the #WriteAngle poetry competition that inspired it.

Thank you Heather, for letting me know that competition even existed, and motivating me to keep at it.

Thanks to all the dear friends who took part in our poetry nights and games of D&D (both during, and after the pandemic) for inspiring many of the poems contained within.

Most importantly, my thanks to you, reading this now, for enabling my delusions that this is in any way like publishing a real book. Maybe someday, eh?

PREFACE

Of the following poems, just over half were specifically written for the contest. The rest are simply poems I enjoyed writing and sharing in the past, but I hope you enjoy the read regardless.

Contents

Beach (2020)

When I was tiny,
They'd take me to the beach.
They'd carry me from the car,
Swaddled tight in a bundle
And stroll down to the shore
So they could show me the world.
I had no clue what it meant,
But their faces were bright smiles,
Happy and peaceful,
So I smiled back in return.
I waved my fat little fists at the seagulls,
While they talked about the future
And everything out there
That was waiting for me.
It grew cold, and I grew fussy, but I had seen it
And that had been enough for them.

When I was small,
They'd take me to the beach.
Some children are fascinated by the sea,
But not me.
I cared more about dropping my ice cream
In the sand.

We'd spend hours,
Dooming cones and combing dunes,
But we'd end up eventually standing there
In the foam.
I'd take stumbling steps through the surf
And the seaweed,
But I was never really standing, not really.
I was firmly anchored at the wrists,
Safe to pretend
But I knew I'd be whisked ashore,
If my footing should ever falter.

When I was bigger,
We'd go to the beach.
Before the car had even stopped,
I'd be charging headlong
Into the almost-breaking waves,
Then retreating
To be told how brave I had been.
I'd paddle and swim in the shallows for hours
Until the tide changed,
And I was pushed downshore.
Finding my way back
On those occasions was scary,
Through the sprawling spread
Of people and parasols
But I was brave; I had conquered the seas,
And the picnic blanket
Would be waiting when I did.

When I thought I was big,
We'd go to the beach
Despite my tireless protests.
I'd play games from my towel,
Reject weather and waves,
With a face like the wettest weekend.
I'd be forced in the end
To abandon my gadgets
And engage with the reason we'd come.
But the sea held no interest,
I'd seen all it could offer.
And I'd go searching for rock pools instead.
I'd peer, craning, through crevices,
My back turned on the sea,
And play god to the gobies and crabs.
A reluctant compromise;
Ocean-adjacent at best.

When I knew I was big,
I'd go to the beach.
I'd cast my nets back
And dredge up cherished memories
Of this place, or another much like it.
I'd smile, though I'd read all about
Great whites and jellyfish,
Undertow,
Riptides,
Tsunamis and shipwrecks.

But they were things that happened to
Somebody Else
And I knew I was smart enough
To escape unscathed
If I should ever encounter one.
This beach and this seascape,
For all of their dangers,
Would now and forever be mine to enjoy.

When I was definitely big, surely,
I'd go to the beach.
Sometimes late in the day,
Sometimes before it had begun,
I'd paralyse myself on a rock
And stare out across the water.
Everyone knew someone
Eaten by sharks, now.
All of our cousins
Had been capsized by currents,
Our high school sweethearts
Sucked under by square waves.
Between the Atlantic and the Pacific
Lies the Baader-Meinhof.
I told myself this, because I had to
So I might continue to stare
And feel anything but dread.

Now that I'm big,
I can no longer see the beach.
I splash vividly in my memories, happy
On the surface
But don't remember wading out,
And leaving the shore behind.
All of this kicking is second nature, now,
As a primary producer, an apex prey animal
Adapted to struggle and drift alike.
My only salvation, this floatation fixation,
Keeping my head held up over the line.
Bread and water, essentials,
The only things left
As I strain salt-seared eyes
Seeking land, or an end to my voyage.

The Secret King (2009)

Some day, many years from now,
When lines and wrinkles crease my brow,
I'll sit content and feel a glow,
Recalling where I used to go.

I'd sit upon the cliffs at dawn,
And usher in the golden morn.
I'd look around, and smile to see
How Plymouth Hoe would welcome me.

How every cliff-face, towering tall,
Could never fail but to enthral,
How I felt cheered by just the sight
Of lapping waters, dappled bright.

There on the shores of Plymouth Sound,
I found a patch of sacred ground.
In time, I called that place my own;
Its craggy peaks, my kingly throne.

My subjects: wildlife, great and small;
I had a kindly word for all.
Seagulls brought me bits of chip
(Which must have given forks the slip.)

While Pigeons brought me many things:
Flotsam, jetsam, bits of string.
The sea seemed also to adore
The sight of me upon its shore.

I'd give the cliffs a friendly pat,
They'd wink at me, and I'd smile back.
And so you see, no words suffice
To name my realm but paradise!

For months on end, I ruled that land,
From coastal heights to gravelled sand.
My kingdom thrived, and would rejoice,
When it saw me, or heard my voice.

Alas, my reign came to an end:
Three years were all I'd had to spend,
And when those years had been and gone,
The time came for me to move on.

The kingdom bowed their heads to weep,
And mourned the king they could not keep..
I thanked my kin for all they'd done
To make my stay a happy one.

They in turn swore to retain
The memory of my golden reign.
I wished with all my heart to stay,
But even so, we parted ways.

And one day when I'm grey and old,
My body frail and my head bald,
I'll shuffle up to bed at night,
Undress, turn off the bedside light.

As I slide in between the sheets,
I'll think of them and feel complete.
I'll fill my head with thoughts of when
I used to wander, now and then,

Down to my realm to say 'Good day,'
To all that I met on the way.
How I would stand and watch with pride,
And when I left it, how I cried.

How flora, fauna, pebbled sand
Were always there to lend a hand.
When I was lonely, sad or blue,
My kingdom always got me through.

And when at last I slip away,
And someday close my final day,
I'll go to my rest easily,
And know my kingdom grieves for me.

I'll never be completely gone;
On Plymouth Hoe, I'll yet live on.
And evermore, those cliffs shall sing
Of Danny Boy – their secret king.

Mirrors (2007)

A smile in each periphery;
The haunted mirrors taunting me.
As slowly I myself approach,
High fives are laced with self-reproach.
Who today is glazed within?
Which face of three will crack a grin?
Baphomet stares, in effigy,
Post-modern strains he lives through me.
A measured pleasure, well enjoyed?
A life of nothing, half destroyed?
A greying-out to listless glory?
Decades spent without a story?
These words like needles wait for me,
In place of my reflected glee.
So check your face for tiny flaws;
I don't use mirrors anymore.

Living With Landmines (2022)

The cruellest thing
About a life that isn't like it was
Is all the ways that it is.
When what would already have been
A struggle through hostile terrain
Becomes a gruelling odyssey
Through a warzone.
Your regimental responses
Tuned to a breaking point
In anticipation of the next missile.

You'll have breakfast,
Something simple, comfortable,
And stodgy with promise,
And then you'll leave the house.
And you'll turn your ankle stepping off a curb,
Or your eyes will inadvertently rove
Over a van of the wrong colour,
You'll be offered a cup
Of the wrong-smelling coffee,
You'll feel the plate click beneath your boot,
And the blast will take your legs.

All is pain and chaos and fury
Without distinction,
Until you roar back to consciousness
Bloodied, trembling and hobbled.
Staring into the crater
Of the radius you reel from,
Staring into the void
Of what would have been there
But isn't.

You recover, of course. Mostly.
The medic is able to save your legs,
But you're left with the battle scars
And a limp. A twinge in the hip
That throbs at every jarred ankle,
Every red Peugeot Boxer,
Every Irish Cream cappuccino.
You know first-hand the dangers
Of the path you still tread,
Forced to remain at your post,
And the fear sometimes waxes paralysing.

The perpetual weight of importance
Behind each step of your campaign
Squares the weight of your pack,
And you learn to walk on your knees.
Your brothers-in-arms come and go,
Replaced with younger and younger recruits.

Fresh-faced, just out of basic,
Eager to do their parts.
You see a lot of yourself in them,
These infants, these embryos,
Forced unwitting into the unhuman cruelty
Of war.

And as you stand in your crater,
Your exhalations flaring with momentary fire,
Pungent smog roiling from your nostrils,
You say, hey kid.
Another twinge of your hip,
You're saying hey, be careful out there.
And you hope you see
That fire in their eyes tempered.
To see this thirst to charge,
Headlong over the top,
Dessicate and die off;
For this will not be
The glorious Hollywood blockbuster
We are sold.

It will be messy,
It will be costly,
And it will hurt more
Than you have ever thought possible,
If you put a foot wrong out in the field.

And you watch them leave,
These young guns, they stride out of the gate,
With the stars in their eyes;
They're not watching their step.
And you shake your head, reflecting.
Nobody comes out of a war
The same man as went in.
And you hope that life will be kind
To these future survivors,
These bitter veterans in waiting.
You really do hope.

The Dissolution of an Innocent Biscuit in the Milky Tea of Human Cruelty: The Bittersweet Tale of Ranibow Sprimkle - Part I (2022)

In a world not unlike many others
(Though, in fairness, a tiny bit smothered
In magicians and priests,
Dungeons, dragons and beasts)
Lived a halfling and his doting mother.

Now Miralda, the mother, was gentle,
And her pride in her boy, monumental.
But how far she would go
For her son Ranibow
Would eventually prove detrimental.

The Sprimkles lived smack in the middle
Of a beautiful village named Idyll.
A lively wee place
With a smile on each face
And which echoed with song, verse and fiddle.

Despite hearts with compassion aglow,
There was one thing the town came to know.
None could walk in the sandals;
Or hope to hold a candle,
To the kindness of young Ranibow.

And as Ranibow grew, he was shown
How to play banjo, harp and trombone.
How to strum on a lute
And to master the flute
And how joy, through a tune, could be sown.

Though the life of a bard was appealin'
(As his talent was slowly revealin')
It was words on a page,
Tales of love and of rage,
That young Ranibow wanted to deal in.

His passion now clear, he pursued it;
And each verse that he uttered, imbued it
With a power profane,
Unforeseen and arcane,
And without even knowing, abused it.

But Miralda realised he was gifted;
Saw the flickers of magic that drifted
From her boy as he spoke.
And her gentle heart broke,
As the mood in the village had shifted.

Though the realisation aggrieved her,
Fear of magic now spread like a fever.
To ensure his survival
(For she feared a reprisal)
She beseeched her dear offspring to leave her.

And though Ranibow could not envision
Why his mother would give him this mission:
For the sake of her smile,
He could leave for a while,
So enacted his own swift excision.

And so Ranibow strode from his homeland,
With his fate now clutched tight in his own hand.
And he whistled a tune,
The poor affable loon,
More akin to a child than a grown man.

But the world he explored could be cruel,
To a fellow so blind to its rules.
And this trusting young dolt,
Raised naive (to a fault)
Would be made not a friend, but a fool.

Curtain Up (2022)

Home is where the heart is,
That's what they say -
But some hail from homes entirely heartless.
I prefer to say,
Wherever your heart is,
You can build a home.
And home can be lots of things.
A scent, a server, a supermarket,
A sensation,
A specific embrace,
An off-key melody.
Places of strength,
Places of comfort,
And of renewal.
And here you'll find me,
Radiant and gleeful,
At home
In my amphitheatre of conflict.

Always hosting some matinée or other,
I'm treading the boards,
And treading the necks
Of the Machiavellian merchants
And mysterious miscreants

I leave in my callous wake.
As I stride across my stage,
I'm jumping from role to role.
Crossing swords with my co-stars,
Basking in my fixation on the performance.
All but blind, to all but the thrill of battle.
And did I mention?
I choreograph the fights myself.
More of a director, I suppose,
But I'm never happier than onstage,
Blood singing in my ears.

Face to face, weapons drawn,
We're fighting dirty,
A knock-down, drag-out brawl
That we're all trying to make feel real.
It's the rush of adrenaline,
The thunder booming inside your chest,
That yearns to roll and beget
That gets you.
You've never touched cocaine,
But the rush, it's what it puts you in mind of.
Careful.
Your place on this stage is crucial.
And as you pirouette
Through your rotisserie of identities,
Characters enter and leave the scene,
Roles live, and, well - roles die -
You're convincing so far.

It's a heady sensation,
Syrupy and intoxicating,
All too easy to envision
Pumping from a needle.
You need to pull back.
Fight dirty, make it convincing,
By all means, make your co-stars work for it.
But don't go getting lost in it.
Don't go too far.
Folk want a convincing battle,
One that quickens pulses, grips tables,
Makes you fear for the heroes,
And rouses that underdog hope
That in the end, they'll defeat the villains.
And as a new fight breaks out,
And the actors take their marks,
The worst thing I could do
Would be to win it.

Quoth The Chairman (2019)

in the style of Edgar Allen Poe's *The Raven*

Once upon a midday meeting,
While my team were mostly eating,
There I sat on plastic seating;
Rampant chatter left and right.
Though I grappled with the boring,
Head bent low over my drawing,
Still persisted thoughts of snoring,
Snoring as I would at night.
Every meeting, same agenda,
Day by day and night by night.
Nothing changes overnight.

As my meeting distaste strengthened,
Steadily the meeting lengthened,
To a void that stretched out,
Threatening to take all bloody day.
As I felt my stomach rumble,
And my patience start to crumble,
I fought back the urge to grumble,
Grumble "Every damned Thursday!
Oh, the time that I would save
Without this bollocks each Thursday!"
There I sat, with naught to say.

My attention freely wandered,
As my afternoon was squandered,
And the aching of my arse
Was spreading up my spinal cord.
As new speakers kept critiquing,
The respite that I was seeking
Seemed to fade before the squeaking
Of black markers on whiteboard.
Oh, how hard it was to focus
On the contents of that board!
Lots of words, and no reward.

Instantly my thoughts were scattered,
And my reverie was shattered,
As the chairman turned toward me
And asked, "Well, what do you think?"
Now I'm caught up in a quandary;
It's apparent my mind's wander-y,
With the eloquence of laundry
I fell mute and sipped my drink.
Buying time to plan my answer
I too-quickly drained my drink.
Words were mumbled; barely linked.

Though it seemed I'd dodged the bullet,
Still I grabbed my pad to pull it
And to busy myself scribbling
So it seemed I was engaged.
Though I fought a losing battle,
There I sat among the cattle
And their constant idle prattle,
That might never be assuaged.
Still I watched the clock, entreating
That my pain might be assuaged.
Thirty minutes… How I'd aged.

Someone else who had attended
Sought to see the meeting ended,
And I hoped his words of wisdom
Might my sanity yet save.
Though I silently implored him,
Chairman doggedly ignored him,
On a rising tide of boredom,
Still I rode an endless wave.
But I felt that I might drown
Beneath this endless, draining wave,
And this meeting, mark my grave.

Just as things were at their bleakest,
And my resolve at its weakest,
Finally there came the words
I'd feared that I might never hear.
Overriding my derision,
There came an abrupt collision –
It was practically elysian!
Of those words against my ear.
After what I'm sure was hours,
Finally they reached my ear.
"Okay folks, let's leave it here."

I could scarce believe my fortune,
I'd be skipping through that door soon
Off to smoke a thousand cigarettes,
And soothe this meeting's sting.
I ripped out my laptop cable,
Just as quick as I was able,
And I stood up from the table
As my heart began to sing.
Of nicotine and freedom, oh,
My heart would gaily sing!
Quoth the chairman, "One more thing…"

Blanket (2020)

Take this blanket off me,
For it does not help me sleep.
It does not bring me comfort;
And I've cause enough to weep.

The purpose of a blanket
Is to soothe and ease one's shivers.
I've felt, instead, a seeping chill
Since this blanket was delivered.

I did not choose the pattern,
Nor the stitching, nor the colour.
I did not choose the way
This blanket bleeds the sunshine duller.

I did not browse the website,
Did not add it to my cart.
So someone, pray, explain this blanket,
Weighing on my heart.

From dawn to dusk I wear this
Wretched blanket like a cape.
Despite my frantic efforts to
Escape its stubborn drape.

On sight of something cheerful
That might brighten up my day,
This blanket mutely reaches up
And turns my face away.

From time to time I snap and
Hurl this blanket from my person.
Before I've turned my back, a thwack:
It's back, and things have worsened.

It seems I must adjust to life
Beneath this blanket's weight.
I see no signs of respite
From my heavy, woollen fate.

I could not say who wrought it,
Nor who wove its separate threads.
I just wish, with that fabric,
They'd made something else instead.

The Dissolution of an Innocent Biscuit in the Milky Tea of Human Cruelty: The Bittersweet Tale of Ranibow Sprimkle - Part II (2022)

At an inn where he stopped on his travels,
Sprimkle's fortunes began to unravel.
As the hapless young bard
Drew the ire of the guard
And was charged with the bang of a gavel.

Though the lad had just tried to do right,
By accepting the blame for a fight,
The verdict was clear,
Said the judge with a sneer:
Ranibow would be exiled that night.

And thus was he summarily carted,
To a place where, he learned, he'd be parted
From all that he'd held dear
And would know only fear.
And his troubles, it seemed, had just started.

He was shackled, stripped nude and afraid,
In a likewise-found-guilty brigade,
In the hold of a ship,
With no chance of a kip,
As to Wraeclast they all were conveyed.

But before the first glimmer of day showed,
Fortune smiled on that piteous payload,
As a violent storm
(With a blast like a horn)
Amplified the waves over which they rode.

With a crack and a shatter of timber,
The waves battered the ship into tinder.
Chains reduced to debris,
The captives could swim free!
Alas, Ranibow was not so limber.

Wrestling with the bonds that still bound him,
Murky water now rushed to surround him.
Alone, drowning, restrained,
There he might have remained,
Were it not for two strong hands that found him.

And in spite of the seas still a-churning,
Ranibow, with his lungs now a-burning,
Was hauled clear, to a beach
(Far outside the waves' reach)
Where he fulfilled his respiratory yearning.

As he coughed up the dregs of the ocean,
He stared upward in abject devotion
At the figure by whom
He'd been dragged from his doom,
And he fought to control his emotion.

She towered above him (though most did)
Had no hair, only kelp, like a coast did.
And her skin's bluish hue
Was entirely new,
More exotic than Idyll had boasted.

Though bemused, he tried hard to pretend
That he wasn't, lest he might offend.
As he smiled at his saviour
(On his default behaviour)
He declared himself her new best friend.

For the first time, he surveyed the sand
Of this storm-tossed and desolate strand.
At the sound of a groan,
He saw they weren't alone,
As four others now started to stand.

Stray (2008)

Filthy bottles, mottled grey,
Dust consumes and hours decay.
Heaving stacks here take their place
As monuments to wasted space.
A pile of books you thought you'd lost,
Once browsed with love,
Now rimed with frost.
A box of pictures, a faded shoe,
Three pairs of jeans, the knees worn through,
Some letters from a childhood love,
Sit creased beneath an oily glove
While ancient wellies, stuffed with socks,
Lie strewn across a cardboard box
Of antique records, vinyl blues,
Two decades since their final use.
Your children's bikes slump, scored with rust,
Their prams now coddle only dust.
These things which used to mean so much
Now lie here idle, years untouched.
Within your reach,
Yet you eschew
This draughty graveyard,
Where interred - is you.

Road (2022)

I am a vessel.
Constructed and cut from the assembly line,
Crammed between cops and robbers.
A carpool,
Corralled by cowboys and indians,
Cruising through spacemen and aliens,
Girdled by gridlock.
For years I sat,
An oblivious passenger, beside myself,
Parcelled within an unflinching metronome
In the ceaseless creeping jam.

And then, out of nowhere, it ended.
My chauffeur faded and the open road
Resolved to stretch before me,
As I gripped my wheel
With hands that sometimes seemed
Too small.
The journey was mine, now,
And with it the responsibility
For this tiny mechanical frame
That kept me moving.

So I learned.
I learned the value of a rest stop,
Where the road ahead stretched too long
Or too daunting.
I learned the importance
Of a clean windscreen,
When my perspective waned
Dangerously narrow.
I learned the worth of fresh tyres,
Forcing me to get a grip
If I veered perilously close
To the cold shoulder.
I drove, as I drive still.

Miles fall by the wayside,
And I'm paying closer attention.
My sloshing tank, awash
In trauma and nostalgia.
My sputtering exhaust,
Coping and coughing its dirty clouds
Of smoggy black comedy.
Better fuel might reduce emissions
And burn a little cleaner,
But in this economy?
You take what you get.
Dents and scrapes cluster
In thickening scars across my panels,
But I purr on.

I'm a better driver, now.
I follow better lines, take fewer wrong turns,
and seldom lift a finger.
Mirror, signal, manoeuvre.
With these miles under my belt,
I'm understanding better,
Picking up the mechanics,
And carrying them with me as I go.

Even the most reliable vehicles
Break down,
If they don't release their clutches
Now and then.
I've learned to keep a sharp eye
And a practised hand
Poised over my speedometer,
Keep me ticking over,
If I hit a pothole too hard.
A good mechanic is hard to find;
But the more I drive, the easier it gets.

Clocks (The Impulse)

(2008)

Tick tock, tick tock. Clip clop.
Two clocks report in unison,
One runs, one beats, and both are out of time.
I'll fix it when I get there.
Spit at a wall. No-one's around.
It's not decay of western civilisation,
If western civilisation isn't looking.
Feel the sticky words fly from my mouth
And splatter against the stonework.
See them seep into all the nooks and crannies
That don't realise
They've just had thoughts pressed into them.
Words that I don't think I want to say,
Because I'm not entirely certain
I know what they are.
Better to spit them out.

Countless pinprick beads of light,
I'm beset on all sides by pinhole cameras,
Capturing everything, all-seeing;
Omnipresent and utterly uncaring.
Tick tock.

Persistent.
A distraction; the clocks stop.
Not that they ever really stop,
But their beat is thrown,
The timing muffled.
The stillness brings the cold; the air is heavy,
And my body rejects the silence.
The distraction slinks away.
Hit the button, and the tattoo returns.
I welcome it.
Rinse, restart, continue.
Tick tock.
Clip clop.
Movement is life.
Stand still and lose it.
Clip clop.

The crack has widened slightly,
The trickle, swelled.
The stockpile twitches with its sudden growth
(tick tock)
Energy can always be renewed with effort.
A gift that keeps on giving.
The reservoir fills
As the trickle becomes a stream,
The stillness, a catalyst.
It swills around the pilings,
Dissolves quietly against the dam.
Please let it break.

Tick.
A clock argues loudly with the sky,
Tock.
Need the reservoir to fill,
Or writing this will mean nothing.
Need the dam to break,
Or the reservoir will mean even less.
Almost there. Drip drip. Clip clop.
Tick tock.

The clocks are nervous now.
They talk so loud
That I have to bite back bitter words,
But there's no point
In telling the grass not to grow.
Over half-full. I'm impressed.
An aside for another distraction,
And a knowing smile to myself is all it takes
For the reservoir to reach three-quarters.
The clocks have begun squabbling,
But I'm too close to care.
Tick Tock. Clip Clop.
Another few feet, and we're in business,
The clocks and I.
Tick Tock indeed.
I can't see the pilings anymore.
They're lost beneath
The burgeoning ebb and flow.
The excitement is tangible.

Time to stop.

The only sounds now are the
Jarring
Screams
Of the frantic clocks.
Tick Tock. Tick Tock.
The reservoir has filled. The surge.
My god, the surge.
Then change, an altering of focus.
No longer are the clocks warring,
Their discordant voices mingling,
Joining forces to assault my suffering ear.
Just one, its tone near unrecognisable
In this unnaturally natural quiescence.

Casual, relaxed.
A tick here. Maybe a tock there.
My clocks are fixed. My reservoir is full.
Excuse me. The first crack has appeared.

Exhibition (2021)

Behold; my gallery.
No gaudy signs, no curbside allure -
A simple, stunted building.
Blank and ignorable,
An exhibition making an exhibition of itself
Nobody wants to see.
Just me, and me, and me,
And the piece de resistance - me again.
Crammed into plastic seats,
Shoulder to shoulder with myself.
The bits I was, and the bits I wanted to be.
The bits I never asked for, but got,
And the bits I did, and didn't.
Roll up, roll up - our exhausted refrain.
The plea that someone,
Somewhere,
Somehow,
Might just make it through the show,
Drop some cash, and justify the grand finale.
The great display,
Where all of me files outside,
And leaves us sitting.
You, in the stands, and me, for my sins,
All that I am.

Guileless, posed, onstage,
Stripped to the bone by draughts,
And to the core by choice.
All of me, laid bare, to be seen and critiqued.
There it is.
Would you like it? I don't blame you.
But that's the thing about art, isn't it?
You never get to choose. Art just is.
Look at it all you want, the lines won't change.
The colours won't grow richer
The shading any more exquisite,
The subtext any more apparent
Or less unpleasant.
Art just is. And for now, so am I.
For one night only.
Roll up.

The Dissolution of an Innocent Biscuit in the Milky Tea of Human Cruelty: The Bittersweet Tale of Ranibow Sprimkle - Part III (2022)

There a dark-haired young girl who seemed human,
Was eclipsed by the figure now loomin'
With a snout and a tail,
Clad in silvery scales
(Though in need of some serious groomin'.)

And behind them, now starting to wade in,
Came a tiefling: a red-skinned young maiden.
Sharp of tail, tongue and teeth,
At her waist hung a sheath,
That she loudly wished still had a blade in.

Then what Sprimkle first thought was a boulder,
Sat up blinking, massaging her shoulder.
And he saw, to his shock,
This young gnome (not a rock)
Was about his own age, and no older.

Though the atmosphere clearly was tense,
These five strangers, as one, seemed to sense
If they hoped to survive,
Let alone maybe thrive,
Then a team-up would need to commence.

As a creature of endless affection
(And a yearning for friendly connection),
Introducing himself
To each wyrm, gnome and elf,
Ranibow was first met with rejection.

But that didn't bother the lad none;
Undaunted, he made pun after bad pun.
With no trace of a flame
To spark his sense of shame,
For young Sprimkle, you see, didn't have one.

His new friends were all largely pragmatic,
And agreed they should not remain static.
So they scoured the beach,
For what lay within reach
They could use, amid debris aquatic.

As she pawed through the drowned and the maimed,
Lillia, the young tiefling, exclaimed.
As a number of packs
(Lately stripped from their backs)
Washed ashore, and their goods were reclaimed.

As his friends donned their weapons and chainmail,
Ranibow staunchly chose to remain frail.
A devout pacifist,
He would only insist,
The mere thought of conflict made his brain ail.

Caroline, the young human, seemed also
To share in his distaste, if not moreso.
As she seized not a blade,
But a hairbrush, homemade,
Which she tied to hang loose by her torso.

The blue lass, meanwhile, named Tithrea
(With her morals decidedly greyer)
Took her staff and her sickle,
Both unlikely to tickle,
And a thick leather protective layer.

The dragonborn, Froxiros, bristled
With more blades than Isy the Thistle.
While Meloro the gnome
Plucked a bow from the foam,
Inspecting its string as she whistled.

Friend (2021)

No matter how you build your life,
Direct your joy, conduct your strife,
Make kids, make friends, make one your wife,
Among the population rife.
There's always one to whom you must
Divulge your truths, your fear and lust,
Your hate, your love, and though distrust
May permeate your heaving bust,
I pray that you will yet be kind.
For if you could be so inclined
As to engage them, you might find
But echoes of your selfsame mind.
This person, I assure you, friend,
Has dutifully watched you spend
Your every waking moment penned
In cells beside them, end to end.
You choose a house or bungalow
And *quelle surprise*! Look who's in tow.
Feel free to rant, or tell them 'no'
But where you move, they too will go.
So here's my message, ladies, gents,
(If you'll excuse my two free cents)
I offer you encouragement
To strive to love that resident.

Their presence ever will abide
In each abode where you reside,
So rather than try just to hide,
Why not invite your guest inside?
Befriend them, is my sound advice;
Reread this verse to hear it twice.
You'll taste much more of life's rich spice
If you can bear but to be nice
To this companion, staunch and true,
That stuck with you through black and blue.
They've had your back, now have theirs too.
This friend you can't outrun is you.

Things Will Never Be The Same (I've Applied Too Much Ketchup To This Hamburger) (Non-Sequitur) (With Apologies To Danny Sexbang) (2022)

This isn't real. It can't be.
My eyes 404 as I hold you to my chest,
Fingers tracing your shape,
The sensory feedback tiny bubbling farts
Ripped away unregistered
In the maelstrom of my consequence.

This isn't real. I can't have.
A network cable is unplugged,
As I fail to reconcile reality with recollection,
The bloodied hands of my psyche
Defending fruitlessly against themselves.

This isn't real. You wouldn't.
Packet loss merges with loss greater still,
Hubris gripping my chin,
Directing my gaze,
Forcing me to confront
What I've made you do to me.

It is. I did. You have.
And now, you respond no longer.
Blank, absent,
Rent asunder.
I am so very sorry.
You are,
Have been,
And will always be -
My favourite pair of jorts.

For My Grandfather (2009)

When they told me you were gone,
I dropped an air filter.
The glue was still fresh,
The frame bent on impact
And the boss raised his voice
To scold me.

How many times had you raised yours?
To sing me to sleep,
Soothe my laboured fretting,
And hold me in a thousand echoes.
For I am not your only Grandchild.
A single note in a symphony.
The song that may be your greatest.

You sleep, now, in a Badger's bed,
In the State of rest you so deserve.
But you were always away
Traversing rifts, clefts and bars
Far beyond my reach.

One day I will reach, smiling,
To lift you from the floor,
Your bright, clean face will wink at me
As I dandle you on my lap
And your trademarked grin will fill the room,
Glistening in six silver teeth.

You died last year, Grandfather,
But one day I shall hold you in my arms.
And with a slow, sad smile,
I shall teach you to sing the songs you sang
To me, to help me sleep,
When I was seventeen.

Prompted Poems:
A Medley (2020)

On our pandemic poetry nights, over gin and over webcam, my friends and I would usually end the evening by taking turns to suggest a prompt to the group. We would then have five minutes to write a poem in any format we wished, about the given topic.

Those are surprisingly good memories, considering the state of the world at the time, so please forgive my indulgence in sharing three of my favourites.

Prompt:

ARROGANCE

My relationship with you is hatefully complex,
I'm torn between humble, and wishing to flex.
Your counterpart squats on my shoulder to hiss:
'Arrogance is a poison, so give it a miss!'

So even when proud of a thing that I've made,
I'm never allowed to accept a high grade.
It's obvious this was just some sort of fluke;
Any thought of my value makes me want to puke.

My course I have charted away from your borders,
(With fervour that verges on several disorders.)
For terrified am I, that I might seem vain
For feeling some pride in the wares of my brain.

Prompt:

SEWAGE

The torrent of garbage pours out of his face,
And the odour is worse than the splatter.
He stands at his pulpit with pompous derision,
As he vomits malodorous chatter.

In time, we can hope, we'll recycle his carbon.
And tear down his every erection.
I confess though, I fear, that the garbage might win
In the looming November election.

CACTUS

The man approaches, and I think "Prick."
No vibrant green hue to his outward facade;
His waxy skin throbs instead a virulent crimson.
Assurance, adaptability, superiority.
A walking CV of lies.
The only source of sustenance
You could ever need.
The ideal candidate,
And by god, does he know it.
But for all his arrogance, he fails to comprehend
That he is rendered serviceable
Only once cut down,
Dissected, consumed, discarded.
I laugh at his meagre remains.
For a man so predicated on spines,
My grim smile sees none among his detritus.
Prick.

The Dissolution of an Innocent Biscuit in the Milky Tea of Human Cruelty: The Bittersweet Tale of Ranibow Sprimkle - Part IV (2022)

Their outfitting was soon interrupted
As a shape from the tides then erupted.
Ranibow was struck dumb,
As Meloro yelled "Run!
For the isle of Wraeclast is corrupted!"

With a host of small wounds dripping gore,
Rose what had been their captor, before.
And though claimed by the storm,
Here he stood in the form
Of a zombie, now lurching ashore.

And the first was soon joined by a second,
Almost like living prey somehow beckoned
To these corpses now rising
In their numbers surprising.
Perhaps fifteen or more, Sprimkle reckoned.

So the party, as one, turned and fled,
From the until-quite-recently dead,
Ranibow, though quite scared
Was grateful to be paired
With these brave new friends, charging ahead.

Though the spectres had seemed grim indeed,
Presently, his companions decreed
That the threat had abated.
Ranibow was elated
As he lavished loud praise on their speed.

This a hiss drew from Lillia: "Shut it."
As she gripped his thin throat: "Or I'll cut it."
Her point missed by a mile,
Ranibow's gormless smile
Was his only response to rebut it.

As the tiefling released him, disgusted,
Suddenly, a large sand dune combusted
On the path up ahead.
And they saw, through their dread:
There a giant, with great club upthrusted.

The monstrous brute's ambulations
Spoke of violent past altercations.
By the light of the stars
Ranibow saw the scars
Of myriad cruel mutilations.

Though imposing, its wounds struck a chord
With the bard who all conflict abhorred.
He strode up to the creature:
"Hello! Lovely to meetcha!"
Just as Froxiros charged with his sword.

With the giant unleashing pained bellows,
Ranibow stood aside, belly yellow,
Drawing new roars of pain
Came projectiles arcane,
Emanating, it seemed, from his fellows.

Disheartened, he looked on as each new friend
Brought the suffering hulk to a swift end.
Beneath blade, bow and spell,
The poor hapless beast fell,
To an onslaught from which it could not mend.

As he sadly examined its body,
Ranibow spied one thigh bulging oddly.
There sewn into the ghoul,
Sat a jagged black jewel,
Hemmed with stitches, haphazard and shoddy.

To be continued..?

BGM (2022)

I'd say I've tried enough.
Cried enough. Lied enough.
Is it?
Is this profound enough? Sound enough? Have
I found enough?
Do I astound enough? Confound enough?
Do I enshroud enough?
Do I reveal enough?
Feel too much? Steal too much?
Am I real enough?
Am I a mystery? Enigma? Annoyance?
Am I the icon smirking in my mind's eye,
or just some entity,
Tentatively, hesitantly
Wrapped in layers?
A substance. Blank canvas,
Something to define, by definition.
Have I painted enough? Stated enough?
Related enough?
Am I show-room white?
Workroom?
Panic room?
Overreacting, or underachieving?
Over the top?
Under the radar?

Am I visible? Seen?
Or unseen?
Clean or unclean?
Do I imitate life? Simulate life? Stimulate life?
Do I? Am I

Outsourcing (2022)

That was amazing.
I've got chills.
Can't wait to do it again.
I'm watching the arc,
The table dotted with stray droplets,
Loosed in anticipation of a vein.
They find one, obviously.
I've already opened myself up,
And I'm stuck, now,
Awash in their syrup. It's sweet.
As sweet as it is predictable
As it is tainted.
As it's obliged to be.
So why can't I stop?
What purpose does this serve,
That I couldn't address myself?
These unwelcome thoughts,
These questions I barricade against.
Feet planted, shoulder braced,
Stoic in their sticky downpour.
It's not my syringe.
My hands around yours, I'm not steering you.
My thumb on your thumb on the plunger,
This wasn't my choice.
Don't ever let yourself think that.
It was yours.

But it's nobody's fault. Don't feel bad.
I smile and lower my head,
Humble in my magnanimity.
Fully depressed.
The needle wicks from my system
And I let you go.
The rain trickles inside, now.
I thrum with molasses, its fleeting weight
Supplanting a vacuous cold within.
I know it's not healthy,
This little injection of warmth
That you can't help but give me.
But I can't deny that it helps,
Or that I miss it when it wears off
And imbalance is restored.
When the cold ebbs back in,
Bleeding in reverse,
Clawing shut the hungry punctures
That yearn to forgive again.
When I smile slowly,
And I say, 'thank you.'
I say, 'I appreciate it.'
The syrup is gone, now,
Its purpose served,
Its obligations satisfied.
Reeling from your transfusion,
The hollow suffusion
Already fading, I say,
'Same time next week?'